SOME SECRETS OF
CHRISTIAN LIVING

by the same author

SOME SECRETS

of

CHRISTIAN LIVING

F. B. Meyer

ZONDERVAN PUBLISHING HOUSE

GRAND RAPIDS 2   MICHIGAN

ZONDERVAN PUBLISHING HOUSE
847 OTTAWA AVENUE, N.W.
GRAND RAPIDS
MICHIGAN

This edition 1953

MADE AND PRINTED IN GREAT BRITAIN BY PURNELL AND SONS, LTD.
PAULTON (SOMERSET) AND LONDON

PREFACE

THE Apostle Paul tells us that special grace was given to him to make all men see what was the stewardship of the mystery, which from all ages had been hid in God but which He was pleased to make known.

Whenever, therefore, God communicates to us some secret in the Divine Life, unravelling what was involved, or illuminating what was obscure, we are called upon to consider ourselves as the trustees or stewards of others, summoned to pass on what we have been taught.

This is what I have sought to do in these simple pages. It has been my single purpose to tell again what I have seen and handled of the Word of Life, that others may share in it.

But all will be in vain apart from the demonstration of the Spirit, whose office it is to prove these things to the spirit of man, so that he may perceive them by the flash of Divine revelation and spiritual insight.

Life has its mysteries, perplexities, solemn questions for us all. Probably no one can really answer them for another. The spirit must ask its questions of God, and get their solution from Him—in language not always intelligible to the intellect, though always to the heart. But each may tell what God has said to himself. This is what I have sought to do.

F. B. MEYER.

CONTENTS

I

The Lost Chord Found

THE story of the lost chord has been told in exquisite verse, and in stately music. We have all heard of the lady who in the autumn twilight, which softly filled the room, laid her fingers on the open keys of a glorious organ. She knew not what she was playing, or what she was dreaming then; but she struck one chord of music, like the sound of a great Amen.

> *It flooded the crimson twilight,*
> *   Like the close of an angel's psalm,*
> *And it lay on her fevered spirit*
> *   With a touch of infinite calm.*

> *It quieted pain and sorrow,*
> *   Like love overcoming strife;*
> *It seemed the harmonious echo*
> *   From our discordant life.*

It linked all perplexed meanings
Into one perfect peace,
And trembled away into silence,
As if it were loth to cease.

Something called her away, and when she returned to the organ, she had lost that chord divine. Though she longed for it and sought it, it was all in vain. It was a lost chord.

Whenever I hear that story, it reminds me of the lost joy, the lost peace, the lost power, of which so many complain. At the beginning of their Christian life, near at hand, or right back in the past, it would seem as if they had struck the chord of a blessed and glorious life. As long as those notes lingered in their lives, they were like the days of heaven upon earth, but alas! they died away soon into silence— and all their life is now filled with regret for the grace of days that are dead.

Where is the blessedness I knew
When first I saw the Lord?
Where is the soul-refreshing view
Of Jesus aud His Word?

What peaceful hours I then enjoyed !
How sweet their memory still !
But they have left an aching void,
The world can never fill.

These words are written to help all such, and to give them again the sweet lost chord. Take heart! you may again have all, and more than all that you have ever lost. You have flung your precious stones into the deep, there has been a moment's splash, a tiny ripple, and they have sunk down and down, apparently beyond hope of recovery. Yet the hand of Christ will again place them on your palm. Only henceforth, be wise enough to let Him keep them for you.

These are the steps back—steps you may take at once:

1. *Be sure that God Will give you a hearty Welcome.*—He is not an angry Judge. He has not given you up, or ceased to love you. He longs after you. His portrait is drawn by one who could not mislead us, who compares Him to the Father of a loved and prodigal boy, ever

watching from His windows the road by which the truant went, eagerly longing for his return, and ready, if He should see him a great way off, to run to meet him, and clasp him, rags and filth and all, to His yearning heart. That is thy God, my friend. Listen to His words, broken by sighs, "How shall I give thee up, Ephraim? how shall I deliver thee, Israel? how shall I make thee as Admah? how shall I set thee as Zeboim? Mine heart is turned within Me, My compassions are kindled." Read the last chapter of the Book of Hosea, which may be well called the backsliders' gospel. Read the third chapter of Jeremiah, and let the plaintive pleadings to return soak into your spirit. Read the story of Peter's fall and restoration, and let your tears fall thick and fast on John xxi, as you learn how delicately the Lord forgave, and how generously He entrusted the backslider with His sheep and His lambs. Be sure that though your repeated failures and sins have worn out every one else, they have not exhausted the infinite love of God. He tells us to forgive our offending brother unto 490 times; how much oftener will He not forgive us? According to the height of heaven above the earth, so great is His mercy. "Let the wicked forsake his way, and the unrighteous man his thoughts, and let him return unto the Lord, and He will have mercy upon him, and to our God, for He will abundantly pardon." If you go back to God, you are sure of a hearty welcome.

2. *Seek to know and confess whatever has come between God and you.*—You have lost the light of God's face, not because He has arbitrarily withdrawn it, but because your iniquities have come between you and your God, and your sins, like a cloud before the sun, have hid His face from you. Do not spend time by looking at them as a whole, deal with them one by one. The Boer is a formidable foe to the British soldier, because he is trained from boyhood to take a definite aim and bring down his mark, whilst our soldiers fire in volleys. In dealing with sin, we should imitate him in the definiteness and accuracy of his aim. Ask God to search you and show you what wicked way is in you. Marshal all your life before Him, as Joshua marshalled Israel, sift it through, tribe

B

by tribe, family by family, household by household, man by man, until at last you find the Achan who has robbed you of the blessed smile of God. Do not say: Lord, I am a great sinner, I have done what I ought not, I have not done what I ought. But say, Lord, I have sinned in this, and this, and that, and the other. Call up each rebel sin, by its right name, to receive sentence of death. Your heart is choked with sins; empty it out, as you would empty a box, by handing out first the articles that lie on the surface. When you have removed them, you will see more underneath; hand them out also. When these are removed, you will probably see some more. Never rest till all are gone. Confession is just this process of telling God the unvarnished story—the sad, sad story—of each accursed sin—how it began, how you sinfully permitted it to grow, how you have loved and followed it to your bitter cost.

3. *Believe in God's instant forgiveness.*—How long does it take you to forgive your child, when you are sure that it is really sorry and repentant? Time is not considered in

forgiveness. The estrangement of a life-time, the wrong-doing of years, may be forgiven in the twinkling of an eye, in the time that a tear takes to form and fall. So is it with God. If we confess our sins, He is faithful and just to forgive us. He does sometimes keep us waiting for an answer to other prayers, but he never keeps us waiting one single second for an answer to our prayer for forgiveness. It is hardly possible for the prodigal to stammer out the words: Father, I have sinned, before the answer flashes upon him: I have put away thy sin, thou shalt not die. There is not a moment's interval between the humble and sad telling of the story of sin, and God's forgiveness. As soon as a penitent appears in the doorway of God's throne-room, the golden sceptre of His royal forgiveness is stretched out for him to touch. You may not feel forgiven. You may have no ecstasy of joy. But you are forgiven, in the thoughts of God. The angels hear him say: *Child, thy sins, which are many, are all forgiven thee; go in peace.* If we confess, and as soon as we confess, He is faithful and just to forgive. He never says, Go thy way, and return to-morrow, and I will see whether I can forgive. He hates the sin, and is only too glad to sweep it away. He loves the sinner, and is only too happy to receive him again to His embrace. And He is able to do all this so quickly and so entirely, because Jesus Christ our Lord bare our sins in His own body on the tree.

4. *Give up the cause of past failure.*—True repentance shows itself in eager care not to offend again. This care prompts the sinner to go back on his past life to discover how it was that he came to sin, and to avoid the cause. Is it a friendship? Then he will cut the tender cord, though it were the thread of his life. Is it an amusement? Then he will for ever absent himself from that place, those scenes, and that companionship. Is it a profitable means of making money? Then he will rather live on a crust, than follow it a moment longer. Is it a study, a pursuit, a book? Then he will rather lose hand, or foot, or eye, than miss the favour of God, which is life. Is it something that the Church permits? Nevertheless, to him it shall be sin. If you cannot walk on ice without slipping

or falling, it is better not to go on at all. If you cannot digest certain food, it is better not to put it in the mouth. It may seem impossible to extricate yourself from certain entanglements which have woven themselves about you. Nevertheless, remember Him who said, Let My people go, that they may serve Me. He cut the knot for them; if you trust Him He will cut it for you. Or if He do not cut it at a single blow, He will untie it by the patient workings of His Providence.

5. *Take any public step that may be necessary.*— It is not enough to confess to God; you must also confess to man, supposing that you have sinned against him. Leave your gift at the altar and go to be reconciled to thy brother. If you have done him a wrong, go and tell him so. If you have defrauded him, whether he knows or not, send him the amount you have taken or kept back, and add to it something to compensate him for his loss. Under the Levitical law it was enacted that the delinquent should restore that which he took violently away, or that about which he had dealt falsely, and should add one-fifth part

thereto, and only then might he come with his trespass offering to the priest, and be forgiven. This principle holds good to-day. You never will be happy till you have made restitution. Write the letter or make the call at once. And if the one whom you defrauded is no longer alive, then make the debt right with his heirs and representatives. You must roll away this stone from the grave, or the dead joy can never arise, however loudly you may call it to come forth. I do not believe in a repentance which is not noble enough to make amends for the past, so far as they may lie within its reach.

6. *Give your whole heart once and for ever to God.*—You may have done it before, but do it again. You may never have done it, then do it for the first time. Kneel down and give yourself, your life, your interests, your all to God. Lay the sacrifice on the altar. If you cannot *give*, then ask God to come, and *take*. Tell Him that you wish to be only, always, all for Him. We might well hesitate to give the Glorious Lord such a handful of withered leaves, if He had not expressly asked us each

to give him our heart. It is very wonderful; but He would not make such a request if He did not really mean it. No doubt he can make something out of our poor nature. A Vessel for His Use. A Weapon for His Hand. A Receptacle for His glory. A Crown for His Brow.

7. *Trust God to keep you in all the Future.*—The old version used to tell us that He was able to keep us from *falling.* The new version, giving a closer rendering of the Greek, tells us that He is able to guard us from *stumbling.* So He can. So He will. But we must trust Him. Moment by moment we must look into His face, and say, "Hold Thou me up, and I shall be safe; keep me as the apple of Thine eye; hide me under the shadow of Thy wings." He will never fail thee. He will never fail thee nor forsake thee. He will give His angels charge to keep thee in all thy ways. He will cover thee with his feathers, and under His wing thou shalt trust.

But you say, I fail to look at the moment of temptation. Then do this. Ask the Holy Spirit, whose office it is to bring all things to our remembrance, that He would remind you to look off to Jesus, when you are in danger. Entrust yourself each morning into His hands. Look to Him to keep you looking. Trust in Him to keep you trusting. Do not look at your difficulties or weaknesses. Do not keep thinking that you will some day fall again. Go through life, whispering, saying, singing, a thousand times a day, *Jesus saves me now*.

A friend once told me that she had been kept from backsliding thus:—She always took time at night to consider quietly in the presence of God, where she had lost ground during the day, and if she felt that she had done so, she never slept until she had asked to be forgiven and restored. 'Tis a good expedient, dear reader, for thee and me. Let us repair the little rift within the lute, lest by-and-by it spread and make our music mute, and slowly widening, silence all.

If these directions are followed, the lost chord will be no longer lost, nor shall we have to wait until God's great Angel sounds it, but it will ring again in our heart, and make sweet music in our life.

And not only so, but as that chord sounds again in our heart, it will attune our life to accord with these sublime, heavenly notes which are ever vibrating and thrilling around us. We shall translate it into the commonest actions of our lives. All things will fall into step with that marching music, and we shall know what the Apostle meant by saying that our lives may become "God's Poem." (Eph. ii. 10, *Greek.*)

II

WHERE AM I WRONG?

THIS is thy eager question, O Christian soul, and thy bitter complaint. On the faces and in the lives of others who are known to thee, thou hast discerned a light, a joy, a power, which thou enviest with a desire which oppresses thee, but for which thou shouldest thank God devoutly. It is well when we are dissatisfied with the low levels on which we have been wont to live, and begin to ask the secret of a sweeter, nobler, more victorious life. The sleeper who turns restlessly is near awaking, and will find that already the light of the morning is shining around the couch on which slumber has been indulged too long. "Awake, thou that sleepest, and arise from the dead, and Christ shall give thee light."

We must, however, remember that *temperaments differ*. Some seem born in the dark, and carry with them through life an hereditary predisposition to melancholy. Their nature is set to a minor key, and responds most easily and naturally to depression. They look always on the dark side of things, and in the bluest of skies discover the cloud no bigger than a man's hand. Theirs is a shadowed pathway, where glints of sunshine strike feebly and with difficulty through the dark foliage above.

Such a temperament may be thine: and if it be, thou never canst expect to obtain just the same exuberant gladness which comes to others, nor must thou complain if it is so. This is the burden which thy Saviour's hands shaped for thee, and thou must carry it for Him, not complaining, or parading it to the gaze of others, or allowing it to master thy steadfast and resolute spirit, but bearing it silently, and glorifying God amid all. But, though it may be impossible to win the joyousness which comes to others, there may at least be rest, and victory, and serenity—Heaven's best gift to man.

We must remember, also, that *emotion is no true test of our spiritual state*. Rightness of heart often shows itself in gladness of heart, just as bodily health generally reveals itself in exuberant spirits. But it is not always so. In other words, absence of joy does not always prove that the heart is wrong. It may do so, but certainly not invariably. Perhaps the nervous system may have been overtaxed, as Elijah's was in the wilderness, when, after the long strain of Carmel and his flight was over, he lay down upon the sand and asked to die, a request which God met, not with rebuke, but with food and sleep. Perhaps the Lord has withdrawn the light from the landscape in order to see whether He was loved for Himself or merely for His gifts. Perhaps the discipline of life has cul-minated in a Gethsemane, where the bitter cup is being placed to the lips by a Father's hand, though only a Judas can be seen, and in the momentary anguish caused by the effort to renounce the will, it is only possible to lie upon the ground, with strong crying and tears, which the night wind bears to God. Under such circumstances as these exuberant joy is out of place. Sombre colours become the tried and suffering soul. High spirits would be as unbecoming here as gaiety in the home shadowed by death. Patience, courage, faith are the suitable graces to be manifested at such times.

But, when allowance is made for all these, it is certain that many of us are culpably missing a blessedness which would make us radiant with the light of Paradise; and the loss is attributable to some defect in our character which we shall do well to detect and make right.

1. *Perhaps you do not Distinguish between your Standing and your Experience.*—Our experiences are fickle as April weather; now sunshine, now cloud; lights and shadows chasing each other over miles of heathery moor or foam-flecked sea. But our standing in Jesus changes not. It is like Himself—the same yesterday, to-day, and for ever. It did not originate in us, but in His everlasting love, which, foreseeing all that we should be, loved us notwithstanding all. It has not been purchased by us, but by His precious blood, which pleads for us as mightily and successfully when we can hardly claim it, as

when our faith is most buoyant. It is not
maintained by us, but by the Holy Spirit.
If we have fled to Jesus for salvation, sheltering
under Him, relying on Him, and trusting Him,
though with many misgivings, as well we may,
then we are one with Him for ever. We were
one with Him in the grave; one with Him on
the Easter morn; one with Him when He
sat down at God's right hand. We are one
with Him now as He stands in the light of
His Father's smile, as the limbs of the swimmer
are one with the head, though it alone is
encircled with the warm glory of the sun,
while they are hidden beneath the waves.
And no doubt or depression can for a single
moment affect or alter our acceptance with
God through the blood of Jesus, which is an
eternal fact.

You have not realized this, perhaps, but
have thought that your standing in Jesus
was affected by your changeful mood. As
well might the fortune of a ward in chancery
be diminished or increased by the amount
of her spending money. Our standing in
Jesus is our invested capital, our emotions
at the best are but our spending money,

which is ever passing through our pocket or purse, never exactly the same. Cease to consider how you feel, and build on the immovable rock of what Jesus is, and has done, and is doing, and will do for you, world without end.

2. *Perhaps you Live too much in your Feelings, too little in your Will.*—We have no direct control over our feelings, but we have over our will. "Our wills are ours, to make them Thine." God does not hold us responsible for what we *feel*, but for what we *will*. In His sight we are not what we feel, but what we will. Let us, therefore, not live in the summer-house of emotion, but in the central citadel of the will, wholly yielded and devoted to the will of God.

At the Table of the Lord the soul is often suffused with holy emotion, the tides rise high, the tumultuous torrents of joy knock loudly against the flood-gates as if to beat them down, and every element in the nature joins in the choral hymn of rapturous praise. But the morrow comes, and life has to be faced in the grimy counting-house, the dingy shop, the noisy factory, the godless work-room; and as the soul compares the joy of yesterday with the difficulty experienced in walking humbly with the Lord, it is inclined to question whether it is quite so devoted and consecrated as it was. But, at such a time, how fair a thing it is to remark that the will has not altered its position by a hair's breadth, and to look up and say, "My God, the spring-tide of emotion has passed away like a summer brook; but in my heart of hearts, in my will, Thou knowest I am as devoted, as loyal, as desirous to be only for Thee, as in the blessed moment of unbroken retirement at Thy feet." This is an offering with which God is well pleased. And thus we may live a calm, peaceful life.

3. *Perhaps you have Disobeyed some clear Command.*—Sometimes a soul comes to its spiritual adviser, speaking thus:

"I have no conscious joy, and have had but little for years."

"Did you once have it?"

"Yes, for some time after my conversion to God."

"Are you conscious of having refused obedience to some distinct command which came into your life, but from which you shrank?"

Then the face is cast down, and the eyes film with tears, and the answer comes with difficulty.

"Yes, years ago I used to think that God required a certain thing of me; but I felt I could not do what He wished, was uneasy for some time about it, but after awhile it seemed to fade from my mind, and now it does not often trouble me."

"Ah, soul, that is where thou hast gone wrong, and thou wilt never get right till thou goest right back through the weary years to the point where thou didst drop the thread of obedience, and performest that one thing which God demanded of thee so long ago, but on account of which thou didst leave the narrow track of implicit obedience."

Is not this the cause of depression to thousands of Christian people? They are God's children, but they are disobedient children. The Bible rings with one long demand for obedience. The key-word of the book of Deuteronomy is, *Observe and Do*.

c

The burden of the Farewell Discourse is, *If ye love Me keep My commandments*. We must not question or reply or excuse ourselves. We must not pick and choose our way. We must not take some commands and reject others. We must not think that obedience in other directions will compensate for disbedience in some one particular. God gives one command at a time, borne in upon us, not in one way only, but in many; by this He tests us. If we obey in this, He will flood our soul with blessing, and lead us forward into new paths and pastures. But if we refuse in this, we shall remain stagnant and waterlogged, make no progress in Christian experience, and lack both power and joy.

4. *Perhaps you are Permitting some known Evil.*—When water is left to stand, the particles of silt betray themselves, as they fall one by one to the bottom. So, if you are quiet, you may become aware of the presence in your soul of permitted evil. Dare to consider it. Do not avoid the sight as the bankrupt avoids his tell-tale ledgers, or as the consumptive patient the stethoscope. Compel yourself

quietly to consider whatever evil the Spirit of God discovers to your soul. It may have lurked in the cupboards and cloisters of your being for years, suspected but unjudged. But whatever it be, and whatever its history, be sure that it has brought the shadow over your life which is your daily sorrow.

Does your will refuse to relinquish a practice or habit which is alien to the will of God?

Do you permit some secret sin to have its unhindered way in the house of your life?

Do your affections roam unrestrained after forbidden objects?

Do you cherish any resentment or hatred towards another, to whom you refuse to be reconciled?

Is there some injustice which you refuse to forgive, some charge which you refuse to pay, some wrong which you refuse to confess?

Are you allowing something yourself which you would be the first to condemn in others, but which you argue may be permitted in your own case, because of certain reasons with which you attempt to smother the remonstrances of conscience?

In some cases the hindrance to conscious

blessedness lies not in sins, but in *weights* which hang around the soul. Sin is that which is always and everywhere wrong; but a weight is anything which may hinder or impede the Christian life, without being positively sin. And thus a thing may be a weight to one which is not so to another. Each must be fully persuaded in his own mind. And wherever the soul is aware of its life being hindered by the presence of only one thing, then, however harmless in itself, and however innocently permitted by others, there can be no alternative, but it must be cast aside as the garments of the lads when, on the village green, they compete for the prize of the wrestle or the race.

5. *Perhaps you Look too much Inwards on Self, instead of Outwards on the Lord Jesus.*— The healthiest people do not think about their health; the weak induce disease by morbid introspection. If you begin to count your heart-beats, you will disturb the rhythmic action of the heart. If you continually imagine a pain anywhere, you will produce it. And there are some true children of God who

induce their own darkness by morbid self-scrutiny. They are always going back on themselves, analysing their motives, re-considering past acts of consecration, comparing themselves with themselves. In one form or another self is the pivot of their life, albeit that it is undoubtedly a religious life. What but darkness can result from such a course? There are certainly times in our lives when we must look within, and judge ourselves, that we may not be judged. But this is only done that we may turn with fuller purpose of heart to the Lord. And when once done, it needs not to be repeated. "Leaving the things behind" is the only safe motto. The question is, not whether we did as well as we might, but whether we did as well as we could at the time.

We must not spend all our lives in cleaning our windows, or in considering whether they are clean, but in sunning ourselves in God's blessed light. That light will soon show us what still needs to be cleansed away, and will enable us to cleanse it with unerring accuracy. Our Lord Jesus is a perfect reservoir of every-thing the soul of man requires for a blessed and holy life. To make much of Him, to abide in Him, to draw from Him, to receive each moment from His fulness, is therefore the only condition of soul-health. But to be more concerned with self than with Him, is like spending much time and thought over the senses of the body, and never using them for the purpose of receiving impressions from the world outside. Look off unto Jesus. Delight thyself in the Lord. My soul, wait thou only upon God!

6. *Perhaps you spend too little time in Communion with God through His Word.*—It is not necessary to make long prayers, but it is essential to be much alone with God; waiting at His door; hearkening for His voice; lingering in the garden of Scripture for the coming of the Lord God in the dawn or cool of the day. No number of meetings, no fellowship with Christian friends, no amount of Christian activity can compensate for the neglect of the still hour.

When you feel least inclined for it, there is most need to make for your closet with the shut door. Do for duty's sake what you cannot do as a pleasure, and you will find it become delightful. You can better thrive without nourishment than become happy or strong in Christian life without fellowship with God.

When you cannot pray for yourself, begin to pray for others. When your desires flag, take the Bible in hand, and begin to turn each text into petition; or take up the tale of your mercies, and begin to translate each of them into praise. When the Bible itself becomes irksome, inquire whether you have not been spoiling your appetite by sweetmeats and renounce them; and believe that the Word is the wire along which the voice of God will certainly come to you, if the heart is hushed, and the attention fixed. "I will hear what God the Lord shall speak."

More Christians than we can count are suffering from a lack of prayer and Bible study, and no revival is more to be desired than that of systematic private Bible study. There is no short and easy method of godliness which can dispense with this.

Many also suffer from the spirit of organization and routine, which is so rife in Christian

work. We do so much; and we do it mechanic-
ally. We are wheels in the great machinery,
instead of souls, the value of whose work in the
world depends much more on what they are
than on what they say or do. We must keep
fresh, tender, unselfish, and devout. And it
were better to relinquish some of the routine
of life than lose the temper and tone of heart,
which are all important for the redemption of
others.

7. *Perhaps you have never given yourself entirely
over to the Mastership of the Lord Jesus.*—We are
His by many ties and rights. But too few of
us recognise His Lordship. We are willing
enough to take Him as Saviour; we hesitate
to make Him King. We forget that God has
exalted Him to be Prince, as well as Saviour.
And the Divine order is irreversible. Those
who ignore the Lordship of Jesus cannot build
up a strong or happy life.

Put the sun in its central throne, and all the
motions of the planets assume a beautiful
order. Put Jesus on the throne of the life,
and all things fall into harmony and peace.
Seek first the kingdom of God, and all things

are yours. Consecration is the indispensable condition of blessedness.

So shall light break on thy path, such as has not shone there for many days. Yea, "thy sun shall no more go down, neither shall thy moon withdraw herself; but the Lord shall be unto thee an everlasting light, *and the days of thy mourning shall be ended.*"

III

A Keswick Experience

One memorable evening, towards the close of a convention of unusual power, a quiet, eager crowd of some twelve hundred people gathered in the great tent to seek a fresh enduement of the Holy Spirit. The time was spent in prayer and praise, and quotation of Scripture expressive of experiences which were lifting many to the open gate of Paradise.

As I knelt in a retired corner of the platform, I realized that the Lord was coming manifestly and sensibly to many of His temples, for the fact of His presence was attested by their almost tumultuous joy. But in all this I had no share other than to long with vehement desire to be included in the gifts which were being so bountifully bestowed. I was suffering at the time from nervous depression, the reaction from a long spell of work; and it seemed to me as though I were standing in some outer circle, with which I must be content, whilst those whose emotional life was more exuberant, were participating in spiritual communications of the rarest type. At last I could bear it no longer, and whilst the meeting was still proceeding I slipped away through the tent curtains into the night, speaking to no one and only eager to be away on those hills which to so many have been Pisgahs of vision and Hermons of transfiguration.

During the week, beneath the searching light of those eyes which are as a flame of fire, I had put away what had been revealed of the filthiness of the flesh and spirit, and there was therefore no reason why the blessing should be delayed. When I reached a familiar spot, I cried aloud: "My Father, if there is one soul more than another within the circle of these hills that needs the gift of Pentecost, it is I; but I am too weary to think, or feel, or pray intensely. Is it not possible to receive it without the tide of emotion which so often accompanies its advent or renewal in the soul?"

Then a voice, sweet and low, seemed to say, "Claim and receive it by an act of faith, apart from feeling. As thy share in God's forgiving grace was won for thee by the dying Christ, so thy share in the pentecostal gift is held for thee by the glorified Christ; and as thou didst take the former, so thou must take the latter, and reckon that it is thine, by a faith which is utterly indifferent to the presence or absence of resulting joy. According to thy *faith*, so it will be done unto thee." Then it seemed to me as if I took a deep inspiration of that wind which bloweth where it listeth. I opened my mouth and panted. I took from the hands of the living Christ my share, or as much of it as I could then receive, of the fulness of the Spirit, which the Father had entrusted to Him on my behalf; and as I turned to retrace my steps to the town I dared to reckon that it was mine as never before.

On my way to take a farewell glimpse of the lake, it being about midnight, I came on a group of friends, engaged in discussing the meetings of the day and the all-engrossing theme of how to receive the pentecostal gift. They were full of holy ecstasy, in strong contrast to my own recent experience, and seemed astonished at the thought that the same breath of God had not elicited a similar rapturous response as it swept the chords of my heart.

And so we passed through the swing-gate, and by the side of the church, rearing itself above us in sombre silence, and came on the terrace from which we could see Derwentwater gleaming below, at the foot of the encircling hills. The night-clouds were sweeping over it, veiling the stars and descending at intervals in light showers of rain. So we drew two forms together, and gathering close, began to compare our experiences.

All alike confessed their liability to alternations of feeling, and even relapse in the inner life, when the conditions of soul-health were neglected; but they laid a considerable stress on emotion as the test of their spiritual condition, and especially on the consciousness of joy or power in attesting the reception of the Holy Spirit. They reckoned that they were filled of the Spirit, so far as they felt His strivings and workings within; whereas, as I had received Him without emotion, I might expect ever to retain and even enlarge its measure, whether the song-birds of summer or the stillness of winter occupied my heart.

After we had gone round the little circle, and every one had recited the sacred inner story, a young business man broke in somehow thus: "Is there not a danger of your fixing your attention too much on the Holy Spirit and His methods, and too little on Him whom the Spirit came to reveal and glorify? My experience of the Holy Spirit, is that He reveals Christ. It is the one desire of my life that He should make the Lord real to me; then sin cannot tempt, or danger frighten. I am a business man; and if I lose the sense of His presence for half an hour, I lock myself into my counting-house, and ask the Holy Spirit what I have done to grieve Him and cause Him to veil that radiance from my heart." "That's it," we all exclaimed:

"it is more of Jesus that we need. The Spirit is come to bear witness of and glorify Him." Then we bent our heads, and under a strong impulse humbly claimed that we might so receive the Holy Spirit that, whatever our company, or engagements or experiences, Jesus might increasingly become the dear Companion and Guide of our lives.

.   .   .   .   .

Are *you* living in the power of the pentecostal gift of the Holy Spirit? His advent on the day of Pentecost was a distinct historical event, as distinct and as definite as the advent of our Lord to Bethlehem. You are living in the enjoyment of the blessings resulting from the latter; are you living also in the full experience of those which have accrued from the former? If not, you are missing the distinctive mark of Christianity, which gives it a unique position among all the religions of the world.

The Apostles believed in Christ and called Him Master and Lord before Pentecost. In doing so, they bore witness to the operation of the Holy Spirit in their hearts. He had been working in the hearts of men from the beginning.

But there was an immense difference between what they were up to the day of Pentecost and what they became as soon as the Spirit had come. It is evidently possible, then, for a man to be a believer in Christ, and even to own Him Lord, through the gracious work of the Holy Ghost; and yet he may miss the deeper experiences of which Pentecost was the sign and seal. Is this your case?

On which side of Pentecost are you living? Historically, no doubt, you live on the hither side of that great day; but experimentally and practically you may be living on the other. You are in the great light, but you don't see it; you are in a gold region, but you are none the richer for it. Before you stands an open door into the heart of Divine knowledge and power, but you have never essayed to enter it. Whilst thousands are living practically as though Jesus had never been incarnate, died, and risen, *you* are living much as you would have done had the gift of Pentecost never been bestowed. Think! Is there anything in your Christian life that would have been different if the hour of Pentecost had never struck?

If not, be sure that there is something in Christianity that you have never tasted. There is a dividend awaiting you under Christ's new testament which you have never claimed, but which, if once apprehended and appropriated, would make your life rich, fragrant, and vocal, as a garden in May.

There are several tests by which you may know whether you have participated in that filling of the Holy Spirit which is characteristic of the pentecostal gift. Amongst these are the following :

1. *A consciousness of the presence of Christ.*—Mr. Spurgeon said once that he never passed a single quarter of an hour in his waking moments without a distinct consciousness of the presence of the Lord. When the Spirit fills the heart, Jesus is vividly real and evidently near. What is He to you? Do you wake in the morning beneath His light touch, and spend the hours with Him? Can you frequently look up from your work and perceive His face? Are you constantly seeking from Him power, grace, direction? If He is but a fitful vision, you have not realized the first mark of the pentecostal gift.

D

2. *Deliverance from the power of sin.*—The Holy Ghost is like fire. As fire cleanses metal so does He the heart. When He is within the heart in power, the air is so rarefied that the germs of contagion are rendered harmless. When the spirit is filled with the Holy Spirit, it will be conscious of temptation, more keenly alive to its least approach than ever before; but it will have no fascination, no power. People talk much of a clean heart; it seems to me wiser and truer to speak of the Holy Spirit as In dweller and Cleanser, whose presence is purity.

3. *Minute and direct guidance.*—No mere vagary or impulse, but guidance, in harmony with the word of God on the one hand and the drift or trend of circumstances on the other. But we must be more quiet before God to detect it. Dr. Pierson showed me in his study at Philadelphia an arm-chair with special associations. He had been comforting a brother-minister who had been confined to his bed for six months, by suggesting that perhaps God had been compelled to lay him aside in order to get an opportunity of saying

things which in his busy life he was unable to receive. Then suddenly the thought occurred to him that he too was giving God but few opportunities of communicating His will, and he resolved that henceforth he would spend at least half an hour each night sitting before God when his family had retired and the house was still. He said that during those times of retirement he had been distinctly conscious that God spoke with him and told him His will. If you are not led by the Spirit, be sure that you are not filled by Him.

4. *Power in service.*—There is a difference between the Spirit being *in* and *on* us. It is the same Spirit, though in two different manifestations of His grace. Some have the Spirit of God in them for character, but they are not gifted by Him for service. Our Lord Jesus, though conceived of the Holy Ghost, yet stood beneath the open heavens to be anointed of the Spirit before He entered on His public ministry; and the Church was held back from her work of evangelising the waiting world until she had received the pentecostal enduement of power. Yet how many Christians

are attempting to do this work without this power.

When speaking on this theme at a recent students' convention at Northfield, Mr. Moody was completely broken down, and in utterances choked with weeping confessed that he was deeply conscious of his lack of this special power. The whole of the students broke down too, and he asked them to give up the customary afternoon sports and to meet him in the neighbouring woods, that they might together seek a fresh anointing for service. Are we conscious of possessing this qualification for soul-winning? If not, why do you not claim your share of the pentecostal life from your Trustee and Representative?

.   .   .   .   .

We often wish that we could have been amongst the favoured group when the day of Pentecost had fully come, and they were all together in the upper room. We think that we should, of course, have heard the sound as of the rushing of a mighty wind, and received on our brows the encircling flame, in our hearts the blessed filling. But in all likelihood, if we had been there in our present condition, the hurricane of blessing would have swept past, leaving us dry and insensible. Whilst if that pentecostal group were living now, they would detect as much of the Spirit's presence, they would be as conscious of the working of the Lord Jesus, they would find life as full of God, as in the days when the age was young. Peter would still be filled with the Holy Ghost and speak; Paul would be caught up into the seventh heaven, and need a thorn to counterbalance the splendour of the revelations; John would find doors opening into heaven, amid the conditions of our modern life, not less than when the chime of the Ægean Sea rose from the beach of Patmos.

A change, you say, is needed. But there need be no change in your circumstances, in the atmosphere or environment of your life. There is as much of the Holy Ghost within your reach as was present on the day of Pentecost. This is the age of Pentecost. He waits to fill you as He did the hundred and twenty gathered in the upper room. The miraculous gifts have passed away, because no longer needed. They are replaced by evidences that were not possible in those early days. But the essence of the pentecostal gift, the filling of the Spirit, is as possible to-day as ever. "The promise," said the Apostle, alluding to our Saviour's words, "is unto all that are afar off, even as many as the Lord our God shall call" (Acts i. 4; ii. 39).

But of what use is it to live in a very ocean of power and love, if we are unable to discern its presence or appropriate its marvellous properties? Of what use is it that the land of the Hottentots is as full of electricity as London is, if they know not and cannot use its mighty energy? Of what use is it that the summer days are full of dews, and heat, and light, and other materials out of which peaches and nectarines are made, if there are no peach-blossoms nestling on the boughs to detect or use them? Of what use is it that the floor is covered with nourishing food, if the new-born babe which lies beside it is unconscious of its existence and incapable of assimilating it?

There is no need, then, to sigh for the lost age of gold, since the King of all ages is here.

Had we lived with Him in his earthly life, the benefit would have been infinitesimal apart from *appropriating faith*; but if we have *that*, though we see him not, we may secure His choicest gifts. These conditions, however, must be fulfilled before you can exercise that faith and receive that supreme gift:

1. *Be careful that you desire the filling of the Holy Spirit only for the glory of God.*—If you want it that you may realize a certain experience, or attract people to yourself, or transform some difficulty into a stepping-stone, you are likely to miss it. You must be set on the one purpose of magnifying the Lord Jesus in your body, whether by life or death. Ask that all inferior motives may be destroyed, and that this may burn strong and clear within you.

2. *Be cleansed from all sin of which you may be conscious.*—If you have grieved God by impurity, or anger, or unkind judgments of others, seek forgiveness, restoration, and cleansing. The cleansed heart is an essential condition of Spirit-filling.

3. *Present yourself and your members to God.*— There should be no reserve, no locked cupboards, no closed doors, no vault barricaded from sun and air by a great slab of stone. Open every door and window of your being to the Holy Spirit, and He will certainly come in, though you may not be aware of the moment or method of His entrance.

4. *Give time to prayerful meditation on the Word of God.*—There is no such way of communing with God as to walk to and fro in your own room or in the open air, your Bible in hand, meditating on it and turning its precepts and promises into prayer. God walks in the glades of Scripture, as of old in those of paradise.

5. *Then by faith reverently and humbly take the Father's gift through Jesus Christ.*—Let it be a definite transaction. Ask for the filling of the Spirit, after the measure of Pentecost. Dip your bucket deep down into the brimming well, and bring it back dripping with crystal drops. Reckon that God has answered your prayer, and has granted the petition you made. Meet every suggestion of doubt by the decisive

answer that God is faithful and must do as He has said. But specially dare to act faith, going to the temptation in the desert or the ministry among men, assured that you have received all the equipment that you could possibly require.

Whenever you are conscious of leakage; when the exhaustion of service has been greater than the reception of fresh supplies; when some new avenue of ministry, or freshly discovered talent, or new department of your being, has presented itself, go again to the same source for a refilling, a recharging with spiritual power, a reanointing by the holy chrism.

Three tenses are used in the Acts of the Apostles of the filling of the Spirit, which have their counterparts still:

Filled : a sudden decisive experience for a specific work (Acts iv. 8).

Were being filled : the imperfect tense, as though the blessed process were always going on (Acts xiii. 52).

Full : the adjective, indicating the perpetual experience (Acts vi. 8).

The lives that touch other lives resemble

not the shallow streamlet, but the full ocean heaving beneath the great arch of the sky, which sends its pulse along the beach, and far up the inlets and creeks. Be such a life ours, in depth, and breadth, and everlasting strength, because filled from the fullness of God!

IV

The Secret of Christ's Indwelling

It is meet that the largest church in the greatest Gentile city in the world should be dedicated to the Apostle Paul, for Gentiles are under a great obligation to him as the Apostle of the Gentiles. It is to him that we owe, under the Spirit of God, the unveiling of two great mysteries, which specially touch us as Gentiles.

The *first* of these, glorious as it is, we cannot now stay to discuss, though it wrought a revolution when first preached and maintained by the Apostle in the face of the most strenuous opposition. Till then, Gentiles were expected to become Jews before they were Christians, and to pass through the synagogue to the church. But he showed that this was not needful, and that Gentiles stood on the same level as Jews with respect to the privileges of the gospel—fellow-heirs, and fellow-members of the body, and fellow-partakers of the promise in Christ Jesus through the gospel (Eph. iii. 6).

The *second*, however, well deserves our further thought, for if only it could be realized by the children of God, they would begin to live after so Divine a fashion as to still the enemy and avenger, and to repeat in some small measure the life of Jesus on the earth.

This mystery is *that the Lord Jesus is willing to dwell within the Gentile heart*. That He should dwell in the heart of a child of Abraham was deemed a marvellous act of condescension; but that he should find a home in the heart of a Gentile was incredible. This mistake was, however, dissipated before the radiant revelation of truth made to him who, in his own judgment, was not meet to be called an Apostle, because he had persecuted the Church of God. God was pleased to make known through him "the riches of the glory of this mystery among the Gentiles; which is CHRIST IN YOU, the hope of glory" (Col. i. 27).

"Master, where dwellest Thou?" they asked of old. And in reply, Jesus led them from the crowded Jordan bank to the slight tabernacle of woven osiers where He temporarily lodged. But if we address the same question to Him now, He will point, not to the high and lofty dome of heaven, not to the splendid structure of stone or marble, but to the happy spirit that loves, trusts, and obeys Him. "Behold," saith He, "I stand at the door and knock. If any man hear My voice, and open the door, I will come in to him." "We will come," He said, including His Father with Himself, "and make our abode with him." He promised to be within each believer as a tenant in a house; as sap in the branch: as life-blood and life-energy in each member, however feeble, of the body.

1. *The Mystery.*—Christ is in the believer. He indwells the heart by faith, as the sun indwells the lowliest flowers that unfurl their petals and bare their hearts to his beams. Not because we are good. Not because we are trying to be whole-hearted in our consecration. Not because we keep Him by the tenacity of our love. But because we believe, and, in

believing, have thrown open all the doors and windows of our nature. And He has come in.

He probably came in so quietly that we failed to detect His entrance. There was no footfall along the passage; the chime of the golden bells at the foot of His priestly robe did not betray Him; He stole in on the wing of the morning; or like the noiselessness with which nature arises from her winter's sleep and arrays herself in the robes which her Creator has prepared for her. But this is the way of Christ. He does not strive, nor cry, nor lift up or cause His voice to be heard. His tread is so light that it does not break bruised reeds; His breath so soft that it can re-illumine dying sparks. Do not be surprised, therefore, if you cannot tell the day or the hour when the Son of Man came to dwell within you. Only know that He has come. "Know ye not as to your own selves, that Jesus Christ is in you? unless ye be reprobate" (2 Cor. xiii. 5).

It is very wonderful. Yes, the heavens, even the heavens of heavens, with all their light and glory, alone seem worthy of Him. But even there He is not more at home than He is with the humble and contrite spirit that simply trusts in Him. In His earthly life He said that the Father dwelt in Him so really that the words He spake and the works He did were not His own, but His Father's. And He desires to be in us as His Father was in Him, so that the outgoings of our life may be channels through which He, hidden within, may pour Himself forth upon men.

It is not generally recognised. It is not; though that does not disprove it. We fail to recognise many things in ourselves and in nature around, which are nevertheless true. But there is a reason why many whose natures are certainly the temple of Christ, remain ignorant of the presence of the wonderful Tenant that sojourns within. *He dwells so deep.* Below the life of the body, which is as the curtain of the tent; below the life of the soul, where thought and feeling, judgment and imagination, hope and love, go to and fro, ministering as white-stoled priests in the holy place; below the play of light and shade, resolution and will, memory and hope, the perpetual ebb and flow of the tides of self-consciousness, there, through the Holy Spirit, Christ dwells, as of old the Shechinah dwelt in the Most Holy Place, closely shrouded from the view of man.

It is comparatively seldom that we go into these deeper departments of our being. We are content to live the superficial life of sense. We eat, we drink, we sleep; we give ourselves to enjoy the lust of the flesh, the lust of the eyes, and the pride of life; we fulfil the desires of the flesh and of the mind. Or we abandon ourselves to the pursuit of knowledge and culture, of science and art; we reason, speculate, argue; we make short incursions into the realm of morals, that sense of right and wrong which is part of the make-up of men. But we have too slight an acquaintance with the deeper and more mysterious chamber of the spirit. Now this is why the majority of believers are so insensible of their Divine and wonderful Resident, who makes the regenerated spirit His abode.

It is to be accepted by faith.—We repeat here our constant mistake about the things of God.

We try to feel them. If we feel them, we believe them; otherwise we take no account of them. We reverse the Divine order. We say, *feeling*, FAITH, FACT. God says, FACT, FAITH, *feeling*. With Him feeling is of small account—He only asks us to be willing to accept His own Word, and to cling to it because He has spoken it, in entire disregard of what we may feel.

I am distinctly told that Christ, though He is on the Throne in His ascended glory, is also within me by the Holy Ghost. I confess I do not feel Him there. Often amid the assault of temptation or the fury of the storm that sweeps over the surface of my nature, I cannot detect His form or hear Him say, "It is I." But I dare to believe He is there: not without me, but within: not as a transient sojourner for a night, but as a perpetual inmate: not altered by my changes from earnestness to lethargy, from the summer of love to the winter of despondency, but always and unchangeably the same. And I say again and again, "Jesus, Thou art here. I am not worthy that Thou shouldest abide under my roof; but Thou hast

E

come. Assert Thyself. Put down all rule, and authority, and power. Come out of Thy secret chamber, and possess all that is within me, that it may bless Thy holy name."

Catherine of Siena at one time spent three days in a solitary retreat, praying for a greater fullness and joy of the Divine presence. Instead of this it seemed as though legions of wicked spirits assailed her with blasphemous thoughts and evil suggestions.

At length, a great light appeared to descend from above. The devils fled, and the Lord Jesus conversed with her. Catherine asked Him, "Lord, where wert Thou when my heart was so tormented?" "I was in thy heart," He answered. "O Lord, Thou art everlasting truth," she replied, "and I humbly bow before Thy word; but how can I believe that Thou wast in my heart when it was filled with such detestable thoughts?" "Did these thoughts give thee pleasure or pain?" He asked. "An exceeding pain and sadness," was her reply. To whom the Lord said, "Thou wast in woe and sadness because I was in the midst of thy heart. My presence it was which rendered those thoughts insupportable to thee. When the period I had determined for the duration of the combat had elapsed, I sent forth the beams of My light, and the shades of hell were dispelled, because they cannot resist that light."

2. *The Glory of this Mystery.*—When God's secrets break open, they do so in glory. The wealth of the root hidden in the ground is revealed in the hues of orchid, or scent of rose. The hidden beauty of a beam of light is unravelled in the sevenfold colour of the rainbow. The swarming, infinitesimal life of Southern seas breaks into waves of phosphorescence when cleft by the keel of the ship. And whenever the unseen world has revealed itself to mortal eyes, it has been in glory. It was especially so at the Transfiguration, when the Lord's nature broke from the strong restraint within which He confined it, and revealed itself to the eye of man. "His face did shine as the sun, and His garments became white as the light."

So, when we accept the fact of His existence within us deeper than our own, and make it one of the aims of our life to draw on it and develop it, we shall be conscious of a glory transfiguring our life and irradiating ordinary things, such as will make earth, with its commonest engagements, like as the vestibule of heaven.

The wife of Jonathan Edwards had been the subject of great fluctuations in religious experience and frequent depression, till she came to the point of renouncing the world, and yielding herself up to be possessed by these mighty truths. But so soon as this was the case, a marvellous change took place. She began to experience a constant, uninterrupted rest; sweet peace and serenity of soul; a continual rejoicing in all the works of God's hands, whether of nature or of daily providence; a wonderful access to God by prayer, as it were seeing Him and immediately conversing with Him; all tears wiped away; all former troubles and sorrows of life forgotten, excepting grief for past sins, and for the dishonour done to Christ in the world; a daily sensible doing and suffering everything for God, and doing all with a continual uninterrupted cheerfulness, peace, and joy.

Such glory—the certain pledge of the glory to be revealed—is within reach of each reader of these lines, who will dare day by day to reckon that Christ lives within and will be content to die to the energies and promptings of the self-life, that so there may be room for the Christ life to reveal itself. "I have been crucified," said the greatest human teacher of this Divine art: "Christ liveth in me; I live by faith in the Son of God."

3. *The Riches of the Glory of this Mystery.*— When this mystery, or secret, of the Divine life in man is apprehended and made use of, it gives great wealth to life. If all the treasures of wisdom, knowledge, power, and grace reside in Jesus, and He is become the cherished and honoured resident of our nature, it is clear that we also must be greatly enriched. It is like a poor man having a millionaire friend come to live with him.

There are riches of patience.—Life is not easy to any of us. No branch escapes the pruning-knife, no jewel the wheel, no child the rod. People tyrannise over and vex us almost beyond endurance; circumstances strain us till the chords of our hearts threaten to snap; our nervous system is overtaxed by the rush and competition of our times. Indeed we have need of patience!

Never to relax the self-watch; never to indulge in unkind or thoughtless criticism of others; never to utter the hasty word, or permit the sharp retort; never to complain, except to God; never to permit hard and distrustful thoughts to lodge within the soul; to be always more thoughtful of others than of self; to detect the one blue spot in the clouded sky; to be on the alert to find an excuse for those who are forward and awkward; to suffer the aches and pains, the privations and trials of life, sweetly, submissively, trustfully; to drink the bitter cup, with the eye fixed on the Father's face, without a murmur or complaint: this needs patience, which mere stoicism could never give.

And we cannot live such a life till we have learnt to avail ourselves of the riches of the indwelling Christ. The beloved Apostle speaks of being a partaker of the patience which is in

Jesus (Rev. i. 9). So may we be. That calm, unmurmuring, unreviling patience, which made the lamb of God dumb before his shearers, is ours. Robert Hall was once overheard saying, amid the heat of an argument, "Calm me, O Lamb of God!" But we may go further, and say, "Lord Jesus, let Thy patience arise in me, as a spring of fresh water in a briny sea."

There are riches of grace.—Alone among the great cities of the world, Jerusalem had no river. But the glorious Lord was in the midst of her, and He became a place of broad rivers and streams, supplying from Himself all that rivers gave to cities, at the foot of whose walls the welcome waters lapped (Isa. xxxiii. 21).

This is a picture of what we have, who dare to reckon the indwelling of "our glorious Lord," as King, Lawgiver, and Saviour. He makes all grace to abound towards us, so that we have a sufficiency for all emergencies and can abound in every good work. In His strength, ever rising up within us, we are able to do as much as those who are dowered with the greatest mental and natural gifts, and we escape the temptations to vainglory and pride by which they are beset.

The grace of purity and self-control, of fervent prayer and understanding in the Scriptures, of love for men and zeal for God, of lowliness and meekness, of gentleness and goodness—all is in Christ; and if Christ is in us, all is ours also. Oh, that we would dare to believe it, and draw on it, letting down the pitcher of faith into the deep well of Christ's indwelling, opened within us by the Holy Ghost!

It is impossible, in these brief limits, to elaborate further this wonderful thought. But if only we would meet every call, difficulty, and trial, *not* saying as we so often do, "I shall never be able to go through it": but saying, "I cannot; but Christ is in me, and He can," we should find that all trials were intended to reveal and unfold the wealth hidden within us, until Christ was literally formed within us, and His life manifested in our mortal body (2 Cor. iv. 10).

(1) Be still each day for a short time, sitting before God in meditation, and ask the Holy Spirit to reveal to you the truth of Christ's indwelling. Ask God to be pleased to make known to *you* what is the riches of the glory of this mystery (Col. i. 27).

(2) Reverence your nature as the temple of the indwelling Lord. As the Eastern unbares his feet, and the Western his head, on entering the precincts of a temple, so be very careful of aught that would defile the body or soil the soul. No beasts must herd in the temple courts. Get Christ to drive them out. "Know ye not that ye are a temple of God? The temple of God is holy and such are ye."

(3) Hate your own life. "If any man hateth not his own life," said the Lord, "he cannot be My disciple" (Luke xiv. 26). And the word translated "life" is *soul*, the seat and centre of the self-life with its restless energies and activities, its choices and decisions, its ceaseless strivings at independence and leadership. This is the greatest hindrance to our enjoyment of the indwelling Christ. If we will acquire the

habit of saying "No," not only to our bad but to our good self; if we will daily deliver ourselves up to death for Jesus's sake; if we will take up our cross and follow the Master, though it be to His grave, we shall become increasingly conscious of being possessed by a richer, deeper, Diviner life than our own.

(4) Dwell deep. There is a depth of life in each Christian soul which is too seldom brought into use. We live too much on the surface, and know but little of the depth that lieth under.

It is related of a slave, pining for freedom, that he discovered a mine, from which he brought ore enough to purchase his freedom. Then it seemed exhausted, and he was threatened with starvation. But returning to it, he suddenly became aware of the glistening of metal in a fresh direction to that in which he had been working. He again took up pick-axe and spade, and followed the new lode, which led him deep into the earth, but made him rich.

Thus in the depths of the spirit's life, where Jesus lives by the Spirit, there are resources

which would enrich existence with a new
energy, a fuller life, an intenser enthusiasm;
they are nominally ours by possession, they
may become practically ours by use and
dwelling deep.

V

The Secret of Guidance

MANY children of God are so deeply exercised on the matter of guidance that it may be helpful to give a few suggestions as to knowing the way in which our Father would have us walk, and the work He would have us do. The importance of the subject cannot be exaggerated; so much of our power and peace consists in knowing where God would have us be, and in being just there.

The manna only falls where the cloudy pillar broods; but it is certain to be found on the sands, which a few hours ago were glistening in the flashing light of the heavenly fire, and are now shadowed by the fleecy canopy of cloud. If we are precisely where our heavenly Father would have us to be, we are perfectly sure that He will provide food and raiment, and everything beside. When He sends His servants to Cherith, He will make even the ravens to bring them food.

How much of our Christian work has been abortive, because we have perished in initiating it for ourselves, instead of ascertaining what God was doing, and where He required our presence. We dream bright dreams of success. We try and command it. We call to our aid all kinds of expedients, questionable or otherwise. And at last we turn back, disheartened and ashamed, like children who are torn and scratched by the brambles, and soiled by the quagmire. None of this had come about, if only we had been, from the first, under God's unerring guidance. He might test us, but He could not allow us to mistake.

Naturally, the child of God, longing to know his Father's will, turns to the sacred Book, and refreshes his confidence by noticing how in all ages God has guided those who dared to trust Him up to the very hilt, but who, at the time, must have been as perplexed as we are often now. We know how Abraham left kindred and country, and started, with no other guide than God, across the trackless desert to a land which he knew not. We know how for forty years the Israelites were led through the peninsula of Sinai, with its labyrinths of red sand-stone and its wastes of sand. We know how Joshua, in entering the Land of Promise, was able to cope with the difficulties of an unknown region, and to overcome great and warlike nations, because he looked to the Captain of the Lord's host, who ever leads to victory. We know how, in the early Church, the Apostles were enabled to thread their way through the most difficult questions, and to solve the most perplexing problems; laying down principles which will guide the Church to the end of time; and this because it was revealed to them, as to what they should do and say, by the Holy Spirit.

The promises for guidance are unmistakable. Psalm xxxii. 8: "I will instruct thee and teach thee in the way that thou shalt go." This is God's distinct assurance to those whose transgressions are forgiven, and whose sins are covered, and who are more quick to notice the

least symptom of His will, than horse or mule
to feel the bit.

Prov. iii. 6: "In all thy ways acknowledge
Him, and He shall direct (or make plain) thy
paths." A sure word, on which we may rest;
if only we fulfil the previous conditions, of
trusting with all our heart, and of not leaning
to our own understanding.

Isa. lviii. 11: "The Lord shall guide thee
continually." It is impossible to think that He
could guide us at all, if He did not guide us
always. For the greatest events of life, like the
huge rocking-stones in the west of England,
revolve on the smallest points. A pebble may
alter the flow of a stream. The growth of a
grain of mustard seed may determine the rain-
fall of a continent. Thus we are bidden to look
for a Guidance which shall embrace the whole
of life in all its myriad necessities.

John viii. 12: "I am the light of the world;
he that followeth Me shall not walk in darkness,
but shall have the light of life." The reference
here seems to be to the wilderness wanderings;
and the Master promises to be to all faithful

souls, in their pilgrimage to the City of God, what the cloudy pillar was to the children of Israel on their march to the Land of Promise.

These are but specimens. The vault of Scripture is inlaid with thousands such, that glisten in their measure as the stars which guide the wanderer across the deep. Well may the prophets sum up the heritage of the servants of the Lord by saying of the Holy City, "All thy children shall be taught of the Lord, and great shall be the peace of thy children."

And yet it may appear to some tried and timid hearts as if every one mentioned in the Word of God was helped, but they are left without help. They seem to have stood before perplexing problems, face to face with life's mysteries, eagerly longing to know what to do; but no angel has come to tell them, and no iron gate has opened to them in the prison-house of circumstances.

Some lay the blame on their own stupidity. Their minds are blunt and dull. They cannot catch God's meaning, which would be clear to others. They are so nervous of doing wrong that they cannot learn clearly what is right. "Who is blind, but my servant? or deaf, as my messenger that I sent? Who is blind as he that is perfect, and blind as the Lord's servant?" Yet, how do we treat our children? One child is so bright-witted and so keen that a little hint is enough to indicate the way; another was born dull: it cannot take in your meaning quickly. Do you only let the clever one know what you want? Will you not take the other upon your knee and make clear to it the directions which baffle it? Does not the distress of the tiny nursling, who longs to know that it may immediately obey, weave an almost stronger bond than that which binds you to the rest? Oh! weary, perplexed, and stupid children, believe in the great love of God, and cast yourselves upon it, sure that He will come down to your ignorance, and suit Himself to your needs, and will take "the lambs in His arms, and carry them in His bosom, and *gently lead* those that are with young."

There are certain practical directions which we must attend to in order that we may be led into the mind of the Lord.

F

1. *Our Motives must be Pure.*—"When thine eye is single, thy whole body is also full of light" (Luke xi. 34). You have been much in darkness lately, and perhaps this passage will point the reason. Your eye has not been single. There has been some obliquity of vision. A spiritual squint. And this has hindered you from discerning indications of God's will, which otherwise had been as clear as noonday.

We must be very careful in judging our motives; searching them as the detectives at the doors of the House of Commons search each stranger who enters. When, by the grace of God, we have been delivered from grosser forms of sin, we are still liable to the subtle working of self in our holiest and loveliest hours. It poisons our motives. It breathes decay on our fairest fruit-bearing. It whispers seductive flatteries into our pleased ears. It turns the spirit from its holy purpose, as the masses of iron on ocean steamers deflect the needle of the compass from the pole.

So long as there is some thought of personal advantage, some idea of acquiring the praise and commendation of men, some aim at self-aggrandisement, it will be simply impossible to find out God's purpose concerning us. The door must be resolutely shut against all this, if we would hear the still small voice. All cross-lights must be excluded, if we would see the Urim and Thummim stone brighten with God's "Yes," or darken with His "No."

Ask the Holy Spirit to give you the single eye, and to inspire in your heart one aim alone; that which animated our Lord, and enabled Him to cry, as He reviewed His life, "I have glorified Thee on the earth." Let this be the watchword of our lives, "Glory to God in the highest." Then our "whole body shall be full of light, having no part dark, as when the bright shining of a candle doth give light."

2. *Our Will must be Surrendered.*—" My judgment is just; because I seek not Mine own will, but the will of the Father which has sent me" (John v. 30). This was the secret, which Jesus not only practised, but taught. In one form or another He was constantly insisting on a

surrendered will, as the key to perfect knowledge, "If any man will do His will, he shall
know."

There is all the difference between a will
which is extinguished and one which is surrendered. God does not demand that our wills
should be crushed out, like the sinews of a
fakir's unused arm. He only asks that they
should say "Yes" to Him. Pliant to Him, as
the willow twig to the practised hand.

Many a time, as the steamer has neared
the quay, have I watched the little lad take
his place beneath the poop, with eye and ear
fixed on the captain, and waiting to shout
each word he utters to the grimy engineers
below; and often have I longed that my will
should repeat as accurately, and as promptly,
the words and will of God, that all the lower
nature might obey.

It is for the lack of this subordination that
we so often miss the guidance we seek. There
is a secret controversy between our will and
God's. And we shall never be right till we
have let Him take, and break, and make. Oh!
do seek for that. If you cannot give, let Him

take. If you are not willing, confess that you
are willing to be made willing. Hand yourself
over to Him to work in you, to will and to do
of His own good pleasure. We must be as
plastic clay ready to take any shape that the
great Potter may choose, so shall we be able to
detect His guidance.

3. *We must seek Information for our Mind.*—
This is certainly the next step. God has given
us these wonderful faculties of brain power, and
He will not ignore them. In the days of the
Reformation He did not destroy the Roman
Catholic churches or pulpits; He did better,
He preached in them. And in grace He does
not cancel the action of any of His marvellous
bestowments, but He uses them for the com-
munication of His purposes and thoughts.

It is of the greatest importance, then, that
we should feed our minds with facts; with
reliable information; with the results of human
experience, and above all, with the teachings
of the Word of God. It is matter for the utmost
admiration to notice how full the Bible is of
biography and history: so that there is hardly

a single crisis in our lives that may not be matched from those wondrous pages. There is no book like the Bible for casting a light on the dark landings of human life.

We have no need or right to run hither and thither to ask our friends what we ought to do; but there is no harm in our taking pains to gather all reliable information, on which the flame of holy thought and consecrated purpose may feed and grow strong. It is for us ultimately to decide as God shall teach us, but His voice may come to us through the voice of sanctified common-sense, acting on the materials we have collected. Of course at times God may bid us act against our reason; but these are very exceptional; and then our duty will be so clear that there can be no mistake. But for the most part God will speak in the results of deliberate consideration, weighing and balancing the *pros* and *cons*.

When Peter was shut up in prison, and could not possibly extricate himself, an angel was sent to do for him what he could not do for himself; but when they had passed through a street or two of the city, the angel left him to consider the matter for himself. Thus God treats us still. He will dictate a miraculous course by miraculous methods. But when the ordinary light of reason is adequate to the task, He will leave us to act as occasion may serve.

4. *We must be much in Prayer for Guidance.*— The Psalms are full of earnest pleadings for clear direction: "Show me Thy way, O Lord, lead me in a plain path, because of mine enemies." It is the law of our Father's house that His children shall ask for what they want. "If any man lack wisdom, let him ask of God, who giveth to all men liberally, and upbraideth not."

In a time of change and crisis, we need to be much in prayer, not only on our knees, but in that sweet form of inward prayer, in which the spirit is constantly offering itself up to God, asking to be shown His will; soliciting that it may be impressed upon its surface, as the heavenly bodies photograph themselves on prepared paper. Wrapt in prayer like this the trustful believer may tread the deck of the ocean steamer night after night, sure that He who points the stars their courses will not fail to direct the soul which has no other aim than to do His will.

One good form of prayer at such a juncture is to ask that doors may be shut, that the way may be closed, and that all enterprises which are not according to God's will may be arrested at their very beginning. Put the matter absolutely into God's hands from the outset, and He will not fail to shatter the project and defeat the aim which is not according to His holy will.

5. *We must wait the gradual Unfolding of God's Plan in Providence.*—God's impressions within and His word without are always corroborated by His Providence around, and we should quietly wait until these three focus into one point.

Sometimes it looks as if we are bound to act. Every one says we must do something; and indeed things seem to have reached so desperate a pitch that we must. Behind are Egyptians;

right and left are inaccessible precipices; before is the sea. It is not easy at such times to stand still and see the salvation of God; but we must. When Saul compelled himself, and offered sacrifice, because he thought that Samuel was too late in coming, he made the great mistake of his life.

God may delay to come in the guise of His Providence. There was delay ere Sennacherib's host lay like withered leaves around the Holy City. There was delay ere Jesus came walking on the sea in the early dawn, or hastened to raise Lazarus. There was delay ere the angel sped to Peter's side on the night before his expected martyrdom. He stays long enough to test patience of faith, but not a moment behind the extreme hour of need. "The vision is yet for an appointed time, but at the end it shall speak, and shall not lie; though it tarry, wait for it; because it will surely come; it will not tarry."

It is very remarkable how God guides us by circumstances. At one moment the way may seem utterly blocked, and then shortly afterwards some trivial incident occurs, which might not seem much to others, but which to the keen eye of faith speaks volumes. Sometimes these signs are repeated in different ways in answer to prayer. They are not haphazard results of chance, but the opening up of circumstances in the direction in which we should walk. And they begin to multiply, as we advance towards our goal, just as lights do as we near a populous town, when darting through the land by night express.

Sometimes men sigh for an angel to come to point them their way: that simply indicates that as yet the time has not come for them to move. If you do not know what you ought to do, stand still until you do. And when the time comes for action, circumstances, like glow-worms, will sparkle along your path; and you will become so sure that you are right, when God's three witnesses concur, that you could not be surer, though an angel beckoned you on.

The circumstances of our daily life are to us an infallible indication of God's will, when they concur with the inward promptings of the Spirit and with the Word of God. So long as they are stationary, wait. When you must act, they will open, and a way will be made through oceans and rivers, wastes and rocks.

We often make a great mistake, thinking that God is not guiding us at all, because we cannot see far in front. But this is not His method. He only undertakes that *the steps* of a good man should be ordered by the Lord. Not next year, but to-morrow. Not the next mile, but the next yard. Not the whole pattern, but the next stitch in the canvas. If you expect more than this you will be disappointed, and get back into the dark. But this will secure for you leading in the right way, as you will acknowledge when you review it from the hill-tops of glory.

We cannot ponder too deeply the lessons of the cloud given in the exquisite picture-lesson on Guidance (Num. ix. 15–23). Let us look high enough for guidance. Let us encourage our soul to wait only upon God till it is given. Let us cultivate that meekness which He will guide in judgment. Let us seek to be of quick understanding that we may be apt to see the least sign of His will. Let us stand with girded loins and lighted lamps, that we may be prompt to obey. Blessed are those servants. They shall be led by a right way to the golden city of the saints.

Speaking for myself, after months of waiting and prayer, I have become absolutely sure of the Guidance of my Heavenly Father; and with the emphasis of personal experience, I would encourage each troubled and perplexed soul that may read these lines to wait patiently for the Lord, until He clearly indicates His will.

The waiting is not always on our side alone. God also waits. He waits to be gracious; waits until we have learned the lesson He dare not allow us to miss; waits until we have taken the position in which He can bless us without injury. He holds back blessings which will enrich your life with new meaning and beauty until you have done your full part in the preparation of the soil, and the casting in of the seed.

VI

How to Bear Sorrow

You are passing through a time of deep sorrow. The love on which you were trusting has suddenly failed you, and dried up like a brook in the desert—now a dwindling stream, then shallow pools, and at last drought. You are always listening for footsteps that do not come, waiting for a word that is not spoken, pining for a reply that tarries overdue.

Perhaps the savings of your life have suddenly disappeared; instead of helping others, you must be helped, or you must leave the warm nest where you have been sheltered from life's storms to go alone into an unfriendly world; or you are suddenly called to assume the burden of some other life, taking no rest for yourself till you have steered it through dark and difficult seas into the haven.

Your health, or sight, or nervous energy is failing; you carry in yourself the sentence of death; and the anguish of anticipating the future is almost unbearable. In other cases there is the sense of recent loss through death, like the gap in the forest-glade, where the woodsman has lately been felling trees.

At such times life seems almost insupportable. Will every day be as long as this? Will the slow moving hours ever again quicken their pace? Will life ever array itself in another garb than the torn autumn remnants of past summer glory? Hath God forgotten to be gracious? Hath He in anger shut up His tender mercies? Is His mercy clean gone for ever?

This road has been trodden by myriads.— When you think of the desolating wars which have swept through every century and devastated every land; of the expeditions of the Nimrods, the Nebuchadnezzars, the Timours, the Napoleons of history; of the merciless slave-trade, which has never ceased to decimate Africa; and of all the tyranny, the oppression, the wrong which the weak and defenceless have suffered at the hands of their fellows; of the unutterable sorrows of women and children, surely you must see that by far the larger number of our race have passed through the same bitter griefs as those which rend your heart. Jesus Christ Himself trod this difficult path, leaving traces of His blood on its flints; and apostles, prophets, confessors, and martyrs have passed by the same way. It is comforting to know that others have traversed the same dark valley, and that the great multitudes that stand before the Lamb, wearing palms of victory, came out of great tribulation. Where they were, we are; and by God's grace, where they are we shall be.

Do not talk about punishment.—You may talk of chastisement or correction, for our Father deals with us as with sons; or you may speak of reaping the results of mistakes and sins dropped as seeds into life's furrows in former years; or you may have to bear the consequences of the sins and mistakes of others; but do not speak of punishment. Surely all the guilt and penalty of sin were laid on Jesus, and He put them away for ever. His were the stripes, and the chastisement of our peace. If God punishes us for our sins, it would seem that the sufferings of Christ were incomplete; and if He once began to punish us, life would be too short for the infliction of all that we deserve. Besides, how could we explain the anomalies of life, and the heavy sufferings of the saints as compared with the gay life of the ungodly? Surely, if our sufferings were penal, there would be a reversal of these lots.

Sorrow is a refiner's crucible.—It may be caused by the neglect or cruelty of another, by circumstances over which the sufferer has no control, or as the direct result of some dark hour in the long past; but inasmuch as God has permitted it to come, it must be accepted as His appointment, and considered as the furnace by which He is searching, testing, probing, and purifying the soul. Suffering searches us as fire does metals. We think we are fully for God, until we are exposed to the cleansing fire of pain; then we discover, as Job did, how much dross there is in us, and how little real patience, resignation, and faith. Nothing so detaches us from the things of this world, the life of sense, the bird-lime of earthly affections. There is probably no other way by which the power of the self-life can be arrested, that the life of Jesus may be manifested in our mortal flesh.

But God always keeps the discipline of sorrow in His own hands.—Our Lord said, "My Father is the husbandman." His hand holds the pruning-knife; His eye watches the crucible; His gentle touch is on the pulse while the operation is in progress. He will not allow even the devil to have his own way with us. As in the case of Job, so always. The moments are carefully allotted. The severity of the test is exactly determined by the reserves of grace and strength which are lying unrecognised within, but will be sought for and used beneath the severe pressure of pain. He holds the winds in His fist, and the waters in the hollow of His hand. He dare not risk the loss of that which has cost Him the blood of His Son. "God is faithful, who will not suffer you to be *tried* above that ye are able."

G

In sorrow the Comforter is near.—"Very present in time of trouble." He *sits* by the crucible as a Refiner of silver, regulating the heat, marking every change, waiting patiently for the skum to float away, and His own face to be mirrored in clear, translucent metal. No earthly friend may tread the winepress with you, but the Saviour is there, His garments stained with the blood of the grapes of your sorrow. Dare to repeat it often, though you do not feel it, and though Satan insists that God has left you, " *Thou art with me.*" Mention His name again and again, "*Jesus*, JESUS, Thou art with me." So you will become conscious that He is there.

When friends come to console you they talk of time's healing touch, as though the best balm for sorrow were to forget, or in their well-meant kindness they suggest travel, diversion, amusement, and show their inability to appreciate the black night that hangs over your soul; so you turn from them, sick at heart, and prepared to say, as Job of his, "Miserable comforters are ye all." But all the while Jesus is nearer than they are, understanding how they wear you, knowing each throb of pain, touched by fellow-feeling, silent in a love too full to speak, waiting to comfort from hour to hour as a mother soothes her weary, suffering babe.

Be sure to study the art of this Divine comfort, that you may be able to comfort them that are in any affliction with the comfort with which you yourself have been comforted of God (2 Cor. i. 4). There can be no doubt that some trials are permitted to come to us, as to our Lord, for no other reason than that by means of them we should become able to give sympathy and succour to others. And we should watch with all care each symptom of the pain, and each prescription of the Great Physician, since, in all probability, at some future time, we shall be called to minister to those passing through similar experiences. Thus we learn by the things that we suffer, and, being made perfect, become authors of priceless and eternal help to souls in agony.

Do not shut yourself up with your sorrow.—A friend, in the first anguish of bereavement, wrote, saying that he must give up the Christian ministries in which he had delighted; and I replied immediately, urging him not to do so, because there is no solace for heart-pain like ministry. The temptation of great suffering is towards isolation, withdrawal from the life of men, sitting alone, and keeping silence. Do not yield to it. Break through the icy chains of reserve, if they have already gathered. Arise, anoint your head, and wash your face; go forth to do your duty, with willing though chastened steps. Selfishness, of every kind, in its activities or its introspection, is a hurtful thing, and shuts out the help and love of God. Sorrow is apt to be selfish. The soul occupied with its own griefs, and refusing to be comforted, becomes presently a Dead Sea, full of brine and salt, over which birds do not fly, and beside which no green thing grows. And thus we miss the very lesson that God would teach us. His constant war is against the self-life, and every pain he inflicts is to lessen its hold on us. But we may thwart His purpose, and extract poison from His gifts, as men get opium and alcohol from innocent plants.

A Hindoo woman, the beautiful Eastern legend tells us, lost her only child. Wild with grief, she implored a prophet to give back her little one to her love. He looked at her for a long while tenderly, and said, "Go, my daughter, bring me a handful of rice from a house into which Death has never entered, and I will do as thou desirest." The woman at once began her search. She went from dwelling to dwelling, and had no difficulty in obtaining what the prophet specified; but when they had granted it, she inquired, "Are you all here around the hearth—father, mother, children—none missing?" But the people invariably shook their heads with sighs and looks of sadness; for far and wide as she wandered, there was always some vacant seat by the hearth. And gradually, as she passed on, the narrator says, the waves of her grief subsided before the spectacle of sorrow everywhere, and her heart, ceasing to be occupied with its own selfish pang, flowed out in strong yearnings of sympathy with the universal suffering; tears of anguish softened into tears of pity, passion melted away in compassion, she forgot herself in the general interest, and found redemption in redeeming.

Do not chide yourself for feeling strongly.—Tears are natural. Jesus wept. A thunderstorm without rain is fraught with peril; the pattering raindrops cool the air, and relieve the over-charged atmosphere. The swollen brooks indicate that the snows are melting on the hills and spring is near. "Daughters of Jerusalem," said our Lord, "weep for yourselves and your children." To bear sorrow with dry eyes and stolid heart may befit a Stoic, but not a Christian. We have no need to rebuke fond nature crying for its mate, its lost joy, the touch of the vanished hand, the sound of the voice that is still, provided only that the will is resigned. This is the one consideration for those who suffer—*Is the will right?* If it isn't God Himself cannot comfort. If it is, then the path will inevitably lead from the valley of the shadow of death to the banqueting table and the overflowing cup.

Many say: I cannot feel resigned. It is bad enough to have my grief to bear, but I have this added trouble, that I cannot *feel* resigned. My invariable reply is: you probably never can feel resignation, but you can *will* it. The Lord Jesus, in the Garden of Gethsemane, has shown us how to suffer. He chose His Father's will. Though Judas, prompted by Satan, was the instrument for mixing the cup and placing it to the Saviour's lips, He looked right beyond him to the Father, who permitted him to work his cruel way, and said: "The cup that My Father giveth Me to drink, shall I not drink it?" And He said repeatedly, "If this cup may not pass from Me, except I drink it, Thy will be done." He gave up His own way and will, saying, "I will Thy will, O My Father; Thy will, and not Mine, be done."

Let all sufferers who read these lines go apart and dare to say the same words: "Thy will, and not mine; Thy will be done in the earth of my life, as in the heaven of Thy purpose; I choose Thy will." Say this thoughtfully and deliberately, not because you can feel it, but because you will it; not because the way of the cross is pleasant, but because it must be right. Say it repeatedly, whenever the surge of pain sweeps through you, whenever the wound begins to bleed afresh: Not my will, but Thine be done. *Dare to say Yes to God.* "Even so, Father, for so it seemeth good in Thy sight."

And so you will be led to feel that all is right and well; and a great calm will settle down on your heart, a peace that passeth understanding, a sense of rest, which is not inconsistent with suffering, but walks in the midst of it as the three young men in the fiery furnace, to whom the burning coals must have been like the dewy grass of a forest glade. "The doctor told us our little child was dying. I felt like a stone. But *in a moment* I seemed to give up my hold on her. She appeared no longer mine, but God's."

Be sure to learn God's lessons.—Each sorrow carries at its heart a germ of holy truth, which, if you get and sow in the soil of your heart, will bear harvests of fruit, as seed-corns from mummy-cases fruit in English soil. God has a meaning in each blow of His chisel, each incision of His knife. He knows the way that He takes. But His object is not always clear to us.

In suffering and sorrow God touches the minor chords, develops the passive virtues, and opens to view the treasures of darkness, the constellations of promise, the rainbow of hope, the silver light of the covenant. What is character without sympathy, submission, patience, trust, and hope that grips the unseen as an anchor? But these graces are only possible through sorrow. Sorrow is a garden, the trees of which are laden with the peaceable fruits of righteousness; do not leave it without bringing them with you. Sorrow is a mine, the walls of which glisten with precious stones; be sure and do not retrace your steps into daylight without some specimens. Sorrow is a school. You are sent to sit on its hard benches and learn from its black-lettered pages lessons which will make you wise for ever; do not trifle away your chance of graduating there. Miss Havergal used to talk of "turned lessons"!

Count on the afterward.—God will not always be causing grief. He traverses the dull brown acres with His plough, seaming the yielding earth, that He may be able to cast in the precious grain. Believe that in days of sorrow He is sowing light for the righteous, and gladness for the upright in heart. Look forward to the reaping. Anticipate the joy which is set before you, and shall flood your heart with minstrel notes when patience has had her perfect work.

You will live to recognise the wisdom of God's choice for you. You will one day see that the thing you wanted was only second best. You will be surprised to remember that you once nearly broke your heart and spilt the wine of your life, for what would never have satisfied you, if you had caught it, as the child the butterfly or soap-bubble. You will meet again your beloved. You will have again your love. You will become possessed of a depth of character, a breadth of sympathy, a fund of patience, an ability to understand and help others, which, as you lay them at Christ's feet for Him to use, will make you glad that you were afflicted. You will see God's plan and purpose; you will reap His harvest; you will behold His face, and be satisfied. Each wound will have its pearl; each carcass will contain a swarm of bees; each foe, like Midian to Gideon, will yield its goodly spoil.

The way of the cross, rightly borne, is the only way to the everlasting light. The path that threads the Garden of Gethsemane, and climbs over the hill of Calvary, alone conducts to the visions of the Easter morning and the glories of the Ascension mount. If we will not drink of His cup, or be baptised with His baptism, or fill up that which is behind of His sufferings, we cannot expect to share in the joy of His espousals and the ecstasy of His triumph. But if these conditions are fulfilled, we shall not miss one note in the everlasting song, one element in the bliss that is possible to men.

Remember that somehow suffering rightly borne enriches and helps mankind.—The death of Hallam was the birthday of Tennyson's *In Memoriam*. The cloud of insanity that brooded over Cowper gave us, *God moves in a mysterious way*. Milton's blunders taught him to sing of *Holy Light, offspring of heaven firstborn*. Rist used to say, "The dear cross has pressed many songs out of me." And it is probable that none rightly suffer anywhere without contributing something to the alleviation of human grief, to the triumph of good over evil, of love over hate, and of light over darkness.

If you believed this, could you not bear to suffer? Is not the chief misery of all suffering its loneliness, and perhaps its apparent aimlessness? Then dare to believe that no man dieth to himself. Fall into the ground, bravely and cheerfully to die; if you refuse this, you will abide alone, but if you yield to it, you will bear fruit which will sweeten the lot and strengthen the life of others who will never know your name, or stop to thank you for your help.

Human life is becoming richer as the generations pass, because each contributes its special ingredient to the general sum of good. The leaves fall unnoticed on the forest floor, and rot, but it grows richer. All suffering rightly borne fills up that which is behindhand of the sufferings of Christ, and helps, though it has no substitutionary value, to hasten the redemptive processes that work out from His Cross.

VII

The Trivial Round, the Common Task

A YOUNG friend, richly gifted, but who is tied by inexorable necessity to an office stool, has complained to me that his life afforded no outlet for the adequate exercise of his powers.

His groan is a very common one. So many grumble about the monotony of life's dead-level, which the great majority of us have to traverse. The upland paths, which give an ecstasy to tread, in the bracing air, and the expanding glory of the world, are for the few. For most of us it is the trivial round, the common task. Each morning the bell calls to the same routine of commonplace toil. Each hour brings the same programme of trifles. There seems no chance for doing anything heroic, which will be worth having lived for, or will shed a light back on all past, and forward on all coming days.

But there are two or three considerations which, if wrought into the heart, will tend to remove much of this terrible depression.

1. *All Life is Part of a Divine Plan.*—As a mother desires the best possible for her babes, bending over the cradle which each occupies in turn, so does God desire to do His best for us all. He hates nothing that He has made; but has a fair ideal for each, which He desires to accomplish in us with perfect love. But there is no way of transferring it to our actual experience, except by the touch of His Spirit within, and the education of our circumstances without.

He has chosen the circumstances of our life, because they are the shortest path, if only we use them as we should, to reach the goal on which He has set His heart. He might have chosen some other country—China, India, Italy, or Mexico. He might have chosen some other age—that of the Flood, the Exodus, or of the early martyrs. He might have chosen some other lot—a royal court, a senate, a pulpit, or an author's desk. But since He chose this land, this age, and your lot, whatever it may be, we must believe that these presented the likeliest and swiftest way for realising his purpose.

If, my brother, you could have reached your truest manhood as an emperor or a reformer, as a millionaire or a martyr, you would have been born into one of those positions; but since you are only a servant, a bank clerk, or an ordinary business man you will find right beside you the materials and possibilities of a great life.

If, my sister, you could have attained to the loftiest development of your nature by being a mother, or a rich man's wife, or a queen, you would have found yourself placed there; but since your lot is that of milliner's assistant, factory hand, or toiling mother, you must believe that somewhere within your reach, if only you will search for them, you will discover the readiest conditions of a noble and useful life.

Who can wonder at the complaints of the aimlessness, the vanity, the weariness of life?

People either have no plan, or they have got a wrong one. "What's the fashion?" "What do others do?" "What's the correct thing?" How much better and wiser to believe that God has a perfect plan for each of us, and that He is unfolding it a bit at a time, by the events which He puts into our life each day!

Before Moses built the Tabernacle, he saw the whole pattern of it in prophetic vision. In some secluded spot on Sinai's heights it stood before him, woven out of sunbeams; and he descended to the mountain foot to repeat it in actual curtains, gold, and wood. God does not show us the whole plan of our life at a burst, but unfolds it to us bit by bit. Each day He gives us the opportunity of weaving a curtain, carving a peg, fashioning the metal. We know not what we do. But at the end of our life the disjointed pieces will suddenly come together, and we shall see the symmetry and beauty of the Divine thought. Then we shall be satisfied. In the meantime let us believe that God's love and wisdom are doing the very best for us. In the morning ask God to show you His plan for the day in the unfolding of its events, and to give you grace to do or bear all that He may have prepared. In the midst of the day's engagements, often look up and say, "Father, is this in the plan?" At night be still, and match your actual with God's ideal, confessing your sins and short-comings, and asking that His will may be more perfectly done in you, even as in heaven.

2. *Every Life affords Opportunities for Building up Noble Character.*—We are sent into this world to build up character which will be blessed and useful in that great future for which we are being trained. There is a niche which only we can fill, a crown which only we can wear, music which only we can waken, service which only we can render. God knows what these are, and He is giving us opportunities to prepare for them. Life is our school-house. Its rooms may be bare, but they are littered with opportunities of becoming fit for our great inheritance.

Knitting needles are cheap and common enough, but on them may be wrought the fairest designs in the richest wools. So the

H

incidents of daily life may be common-place in the extreme, but on them, as the material foundation, we may build the unseen but everlasting fabric of a noble and beautiful character. It does not so much matter what we do, but the way in which we do it matters greatly. What we do may or may not live; but the way in which we perform our common tasks becomes an indestructible part of our character, for better or worse, and for ever.

Suppose we meet the daily demands of life in a slovenly and careless spirit, caring only to escape blame, to earn our wage, or to preserve a decent average. Or suppose our one aim in life is to get money for our own enjoyment. Is it not clear that the meanness of the motive will react on the whole character behind it? Will it not be certain and inevitable that the soul which is always bathed in such atmosphere, confronted with such ideals, will become slovenly, careless, mercenary and selfish? And when some great occasion arises it will call in vain for the high qualities of a noble nature.

Suppose, on the other hand, that we do the little duties of life faithfully, punctually, thoughtfully, reverently—not for the praise of man, but for the "Well done" of Christ—not for the payment we may receive, but because God has given us a little piece of work to do in His great world—not because we must, but because we choose—not as the slaves of circumstances, but as Christ's freed ones—then far down beneath the surge of common life the foundations of a character are laid, more beautiful and enduring than coral, which shall presently rear itself before the eyes of men and angels, and become an emerald islet, green with perennial beauty, and vocal with the songs of Paradise.

We ought, therefore, to be very careful how we fulfil the common tasks of daily life. We are making the character in which we have to spend eternity. We are either building into ourselves wood, hay, and stubble, which will have to be burnt out at great cost, or the gold, silver, and precious stones that shall be things of beauty and joy for ever.

3. *The Great Doing of Little Things will make a Great Life.*—Let it be granted that you are a person of ordinary ability. It is as likely as not that you will never be removed into a wider sphere than the obscure one in which you have been pining, like a wood-bird in its cage. Give up your useless regret, your querulous complaint, and begin to meet the call of trivial common-place with tenderness to each person you encounter; with faith in God, as doing His best for you; with heroic courage and unswerving fidelity; with patience, thoroughness, submission.

Go on acting thus, week in and week out, year by year, with no thought of human notice, determined always to be at your best, eager only to pay out, without stint, the gold of a noble, unselfish heart. And at the end of life, though you wist not that your face glistens, others will see you shining like the sun in your Heavenly Father's kingdom. It will be discovered that you have unwittingly lived a great life, and you will be greeted on the threshold of heaven with the "Well done" of your Lord.

Some who are sighing for a great life are unconsciously living it in the eye of God's angels. Those who forgo marriage that they may bring up and educate the younger children of their homes; those who deny themselves almost the necessaries of life to add some coals of comfort to the meagre fire at which the chill hands of age warm themselves; those who are not only themselves pure amid temptation, but the centres of purity, shielding others; those who stand to their post of duty though the fires, as they creep near, are scorching the skin and consuming the heart; those who meet the incessant demand of monotonous tasks with gentleness, unselfishness, and the wealth of a strong, true heart—these, though they know not, are graduating for the front rank of heaven's nobility.

" *Oh! where is the sea?*" *the fishes cried,*
 As they swam the crystal clearness through:
" *We've heard from of old of the ocean's tide,*
 And so long to look on the waters blue.
The wise ones speak of the infinite sea;
Oh! who can tell us if such there be?"

The lark flew up in the morning bright,
 And sang and balanced on sunny wings;

And this was its song: "I see the light,
I look o'er the world of beautiful things;
But flying and singing everywhere,
In vain I have searched to find the air."

4. *It is a Greater thing to do Little Things Well than those which seem more Important.*—They who daily handle matters which bulk largely before the eyes of their fellows are expected to act from great motives, and to behave worthily of their great and important position. The statesman is expected to be high-minded, the Christian lady to be virtuous, the minister to be earnest. There is no special credit to any of these for being what they profess, and are expected to be. The current is with them; their difficulty would be to face it.

But surely, in God's sight, it is a much greater thing when the soul conquers adverse circumstances and rises superior to the drift of its associations. To be high-minded when your companions are mean and degraded; to be chaste, when ease and wealth beckon you to enter the gate of vice; to be devout or zealous when no one expects it; to do small things from great motives—this is the loftiest attainment of the soul.

It is a greater thing to do an unimportant thing from a great motive, for God, for truth, for others, than to do an important one; greater to suffer patiently each day a thousand stings than die once as a martyr at the stake. And therefore an obscure life really offers more opportunities for the nurture of the loftiest type of character just because it is less liable to be visited by those meaner considerations of notoriety, or applause, or money, which intrude themselves into more prominent positions, and scatter their deadly taint.

5. *Little Things greatly done prepare for the Right Doing of Great Things.*—We sometimes lay down the story-book or the history with a groan. We had been reading of some sudden opportunity which came to a Grace Darling, reared in the obscurity of a fisherman's home, or to a Florence Nightingale, or a John Brown, living apart from the great world in the heart of the Adirondacks. "Oh," we say, "if only such a chance would dip down into my life

and lift me out of it! I'm weary, weary of this dull level." Ah! it is a common mistake. Men think that the occasion makes the hero, whereas it only reveals him.

The train must have been laid long before, and carefully, else the falling of a single spark would never blast the mighty rocks, or shiver the frowning fortress-walls. There must be the fabric of strong and noble character, built up by patient continuance in well-doing, else the sudden appeal of the critical hour will knock vainly at the door of life, and the soul will crouch unanswering and helpless within.

If great opportunities were to come to most, we could make nothing of them. They would pass by us unnoticed or unimproved. They would go from us to those who had more nerve, or gift, or spiritual power than we. You cannot, just because you will, speak a foreign language, or dash off a brilliant air upon the piano, or talk easily on the motive of one of Browning's poems. All these demand long and arduous study: that must be given first in the chamber; and then, if a sudden summons comes for any of them, on the housetop of observation you will be ready.

You cannot be brave in a crisis if you are habitually a coward. You cannot be generous with a fortune, if you are a miser with half-pence. You cannot be unselfish in some such accident which imperils life if you are always pressing for the one vacant seat in train or omnibus, and elbowing your way to the front on every possible occasion. David must prac-tise with sling and stone through long hours in the wilderness, or he will never bring down Goliath. Joseph must be pure in thought, and strong in private self-discipline, or he will never resist the solicitations of the temptress. The Sunday School teacher must be regular, painstaking, faithful in the conduct of his class of little ragged boys, or he will never be pro-moted to serve his Master as a minister at home, or as a missionary abroad.

6. *Our Behaviour in Little Things is the Truest Test of What we are.*—If I were eager to secure a good employee for a responsible position, I should not attach much importance to the way

in which the candidate acted on a set occasion, when he knew that he was being observed. Of course he would be on his best behaviour. But give me a private window so that I can watch him in his least considered actions,— how he behaves at home, how he treats his mother and sisters, how he fulfils the common duties of life. What he is then, he is really.

I once recommended a girl as wife to a working-man, because early one morning I came on her unexpectedly in the midst of soap-suds, cheerfully doing the work of her father's home. I knew that a good working-man's daughter would make a good working-man's wife. And the marriage turned out as I expected.

But if this is man's way, may it not be God's? There are great tasks to be fulfilled in eternity: angels to be judged, cities to be ruled; perhaps worlds to be evangelised. For these suitable agents will be required: those who can rule, because they have served; those who can command, because they have obeyed; those who can save others, because they never saved themselves. Perhaps, even now our

Heavenly Father is engaged in seeking those among us who can fill these posts. And He is seeking them, not amongst such as are filling high positions in the eyes of men, but in the ranks of such as are treading the trivial round and fulfilling the common task.

From the nearest fixed star, the inequalities of our earth, whether of Alp or molehill, are alike insignificant. We need to look at our positions from the standpoint of eternity, and probably we shall be startled at the small differences between the lots of men. The one thing for us all is to abide in our calling with God, to count ourselves as His fellow-workers, to do what we can in His grace, and for His glory; never excusing ourselves; never condoning failure or misdoing; never content unless, by the help of the Blessed Spirit, we have wrought out His promptings and suggestions to the best of our power, whether in the gold of the extraordinary, or the bronze of the cheaper and more ordinary, achievement.

Of course there is no saving merit in what we do. Salvation is only by simple trust in our

Saviour, Jesus. But when we are saved, it gives new zest to Life to do all for Him, as Lord and Master, and to know that He is well pleased in the right-doing of the most trivial duties of the home or daily business (1 Peter ii. 20).

May each reader learn this happy art, and go through life offering all to God, as the white-stoled priests in the Temple of old, for indeed, all believers have been made priests unto God: every sphere may be a Holy Temple, and every act, done in the name of Jesus, may be a spiritual sacrifice, acceptable to God through Jesus Christ.

There are fewer differences in our several lots than we are apt to think. Beneath the play of varying circumstances are the same yearnings, sorrows, disappointments, hopes and fears. We learn off the same lesson-books, though for some they are bound in velvet, for others, in cloth boards. But every life may become great, if lived for the great God, and beneath the sway of a great resolve.

THE END